Windows *of* Elegance

Featuring

Glass Reflections
of Fort Lauderdale
STUDIO DESIGNERS

Wardell
PUBLICATIONS INC.

PREFACE

Stained glass has been a passion of mine from the time I first picked up a glass cutter in 1980. Since then I have enjoyed and worked in all aspects of the stained glass profession and consider myself fortunate to have been taught by some of the most creative people in the industry.

In 1989 I decided to establish my own stained glass business and creativity flourished with the collaboration of my associates, designers and our clients. Together we've produced the portfolio of work you will find in this book, from small window panels to spectacular entryways. The photographs and drawings in "Windows of Elegance" is evidence that beautiful creations can be achieved through dedication and perseverance. The design possibilities in glass are ever changing and expanding, and I hope this book will stimulate your artistic creativity to greater heights.

Yarde Harris

Cataloging in Publication Data

Main entry under title:
  Stained Glass Windows of Elegance, Collection Two
ISBN 0-919985-21-1

1. Glass painting and staining - Patterns - Catalogs.
2. Glass craft - Patterns - Catalogs.
3. Glass Reflections of Fort Lauderdale. - Catalogs.   I. Title
TT298.S73 1996   748.5'022'2   C96-931131-1

Stained Glass
Windows *of* Elegance
Collection Two

DESIGNERS
EXECUTIVE DESIGNER • **Carole Harris**
SENIOR DESIGNER • **Crys Soderholm**
ASSOCIATE DESIGNER • **Debra Kasovitz**

FABRICATION
Carole Harris
Sue Cannizzo • Susan Blaszyk
John Kowalski • Mary Ann Schott

PHOTOGRAPHY
Randy Wardell • Carole Harris
Bill Sanders - Pgs: 29 bottom right, 41, & 77
Eli Skop - Pgs: 8 top, 25, 32 top left & bottom
Ralph Weinlaub - pg 9

GENERAL EDITOR
Randy Wardell

GRAPHICS & TYPOGRAPHY
Randy Wardell

SPECIAL THANKS

• To Harold Sanders for his expertise installing these exquisite entryways. • To Norton Canterbury of the Beveled Edge California for the beautiful custom bevels. • To the talented designers at My Decorator Inc., to Alberto Comas Architect, to Fulton Designs, to Jennifer Lang Designs and Michele Cole Interiors, for having faith in Glass Reflections and appreciating the beauty of stained glass. • To Roberto DeMagalhaes for his generous contribution as my business mentor. • To Mike Myers of Island Glass for his undying help and encouragement over the years. • And last but not least to my husband Randy who has enriched my life with his dedication and love.

PRINTED IN CANADA
by Thorn Press Ltd.

PUBLISHED BY

Wardell
PUBLICATIONS INC

To receive our electronic newsletter or to send suggestions please contact us
by EMail at: info@wardellpublications.com or visit or web site at: www.wardellpublications.com

Some Important Information

Window Sizes and Drawing Scale

All of the line drawings in this book were carefully drawn to 10% of full-size, normally referred to as a 1" = 10" or 1 cm = 10 cm scale. If you were to enlarge the drawings to 10 times their present size they would be accurate to the full size dimensions listed with each drawing.

The color photographs are not presented in any particular scale and no dimensions are listed. The photographs were sized to give the maximum possible viewing advantage that the space would allow. Do not try to compare the proportions of one photograph to another.

Stock Bevels and Customizing:

Over half of designs in this book use bevels to one degree or another. Most of these windows make use of standard "stock" bevel widths and whenever possible the designs also use standard "stock" lengths as well. However, in order to fit the window into a specific frame dimension it is frequently necessary to cut a stock bevel shorter or cut it at an angle, then re-bevel the ends that were cut.

An excellent way to cut down on custom beveling charges is to use stock bevel strips. These are longer length bevels, usually 24" (60.9cm) long for the 1" (2.5cm) wide to 36" (91.4cm) or 48" (121.9cm) long for the 1-1/2" (3.8cm), 2" (5.1cm), 3" (76.2cm) and 4" (101.6cm) wide bevel strips. (lengths will vary among manufacturers). Simply use the appropriate width strip and cut it to fit the required length, then bevel the ends with your own beveling machine or send it out to a beveling service to be finished.

Bevel Clusters & Copyright Notice

The window designs in this book are not available commercially as full-size drawings. The intent of this book is to present scale proposal drawings and color photographs of stained glass windows for your inspiration and enjoyment. We want you to use these drawings and photographs to help you decide what you (or your client) might like, consider them as a starting point for you to create your own personal designs.

Wardell Publications Inc acknowledges and thanks the above named Copyright owners for their kind permission to reproduce their copyrighted bevel cluster designs in photographic form throughout this book. If you choose to create a window design similar to one you have found in this book, simply purchase the bevel cluster and use it in your design any way that you choose. We are fortunate in our industry to have thousands of bevel cluster designs available commercially for our use. It would be impossible (and quickly outdated) to attempt to list all the cluster designs and/or manufacturers or sources of supply for these clusters. We therefore recommend that you contact your local art glass supplier to see what designs they carry. If you are unable to find an exact match for a cluster design found in this book, simply use your creativity and substitute another cluster design that is available. Not only will this solve your bevel cluster sourcing problem but in the process you will have created a completely unique, custom window design.

Section Contents & Style Locator

This locator is loosely structured on the style as indicated by the section title.
Some window designs fit into two or more of these section definitions.
Please use this contents page as a sampler guide only.

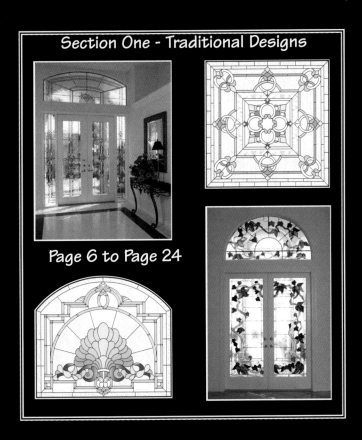

Section One - Traditional Designs

Page 6 to Page 24

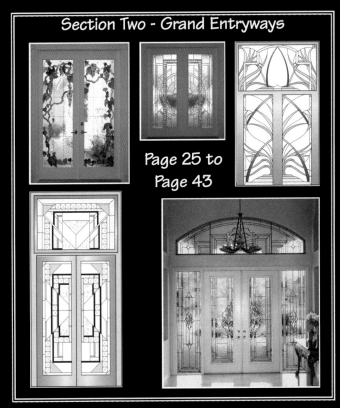

Section Two - Grand Entryways

Page 25 to
Page 43

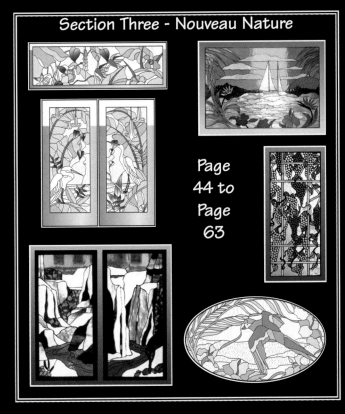

Section Three - Nouveau Nature

Page
44 to
Page
63

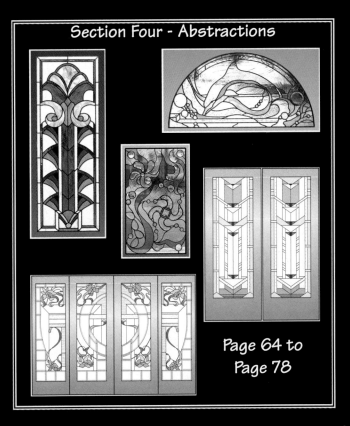

Section Four - Abstractions

Page 64 to
Page 78

Scale: 1" = 10" (10% of full-size)

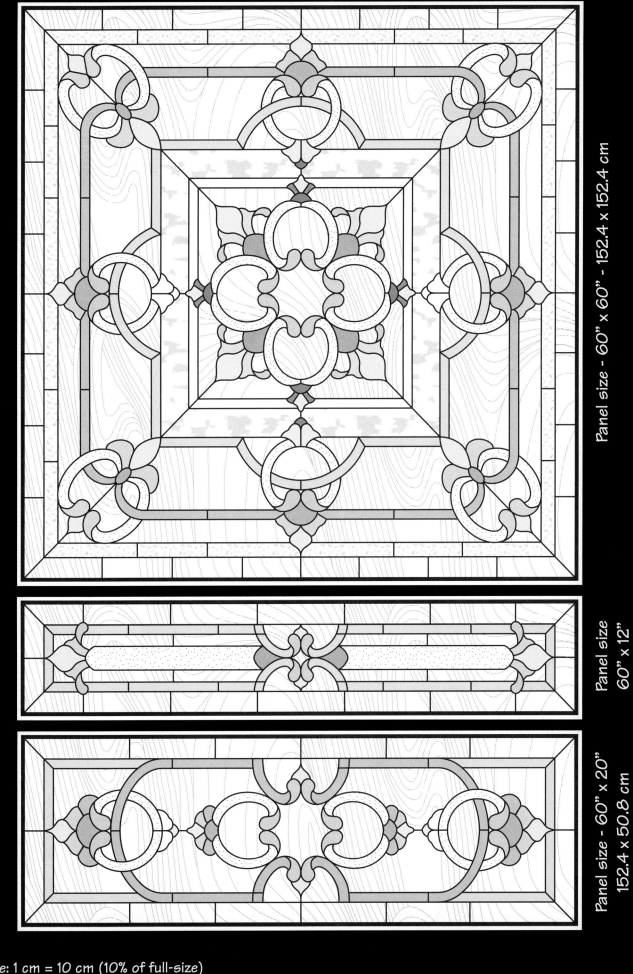

Panel size - 60" x 60" - 152.4 x 152.4 cm

Panel size
60" x 12"
152.4 x 30.5 cm

Panel size - 60" x 20"
152.4 x 50.8 cm

Scale: 1 cm = 10 cm (10% of full-size)

7

"Ornate bevel clusters combined with simple, clean background lines make an elegant statement in these entryways." - C.H.

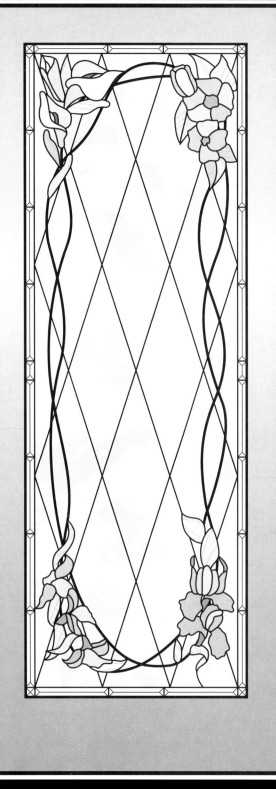
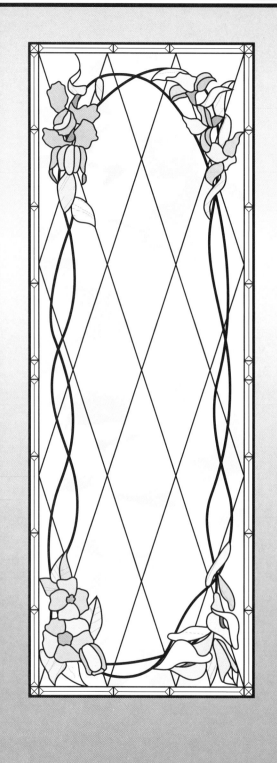

Door Panel size - 24" x 68" – 61 x 172.7 cm

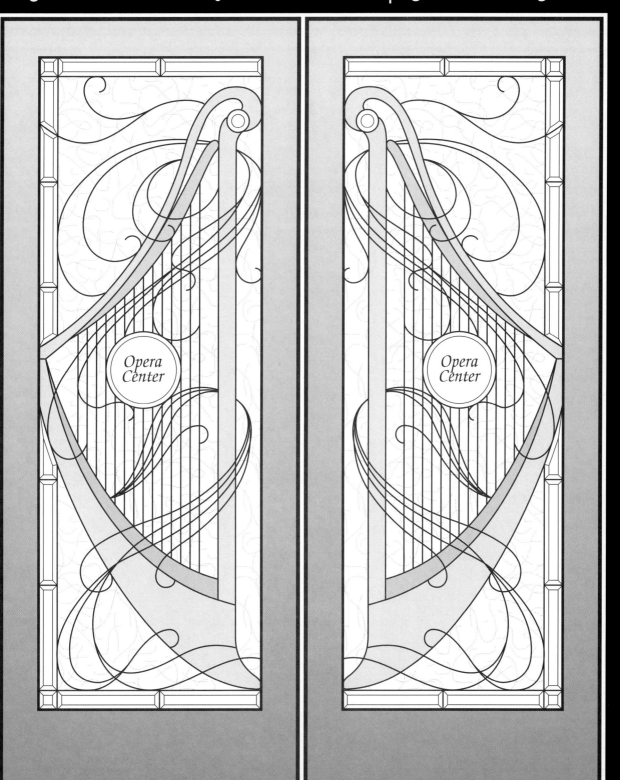

Door Panel size - 24" x 68" – 61 x 172.7 cm

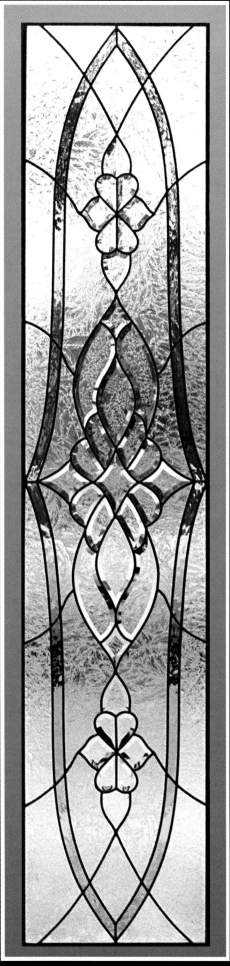

"The trailing vine design used in this entryway compliments the grape vine design used in the den french doors and single kitchen door found on upper page 32, all in the same home" - C.S.

Panel size - 58" x 50" – 147.3 x 127 cm

Panel size - 73" x 17-1/2" – 185.4 x 44.5 cm

"These floral border panels were originally designed to accommodate signage lettering in the center. However, they would lend themselves to a bevel cluster or clear textures, depending on the application" – C.H.

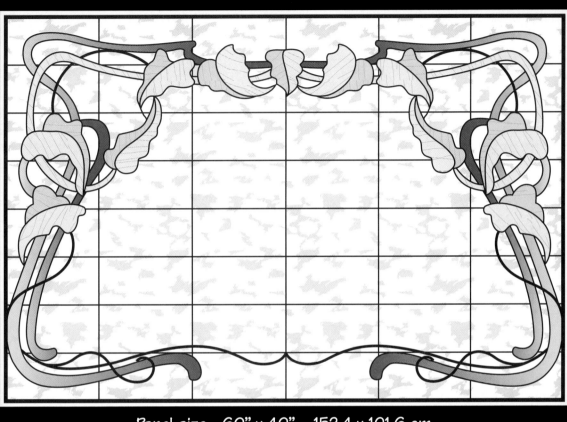

Panel size - 60" x 40" – 152.4 x 101.6 cm

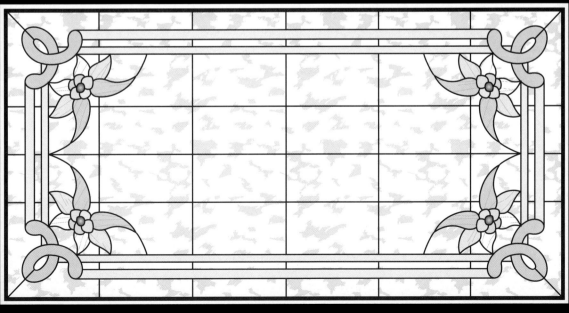

Panel size - 60" x 30" – 152.4 x 76.2 cm

" The pineapple is the affable symbol of friendship and enhances these windows made with blown antique glass." – C.H.

Door Panel size - 28" x 74" – 71.1 x 188 cm

"These two proposal drawings were created for a pass-through opening, to be installed in pocket-style sliding frames" – C.H.

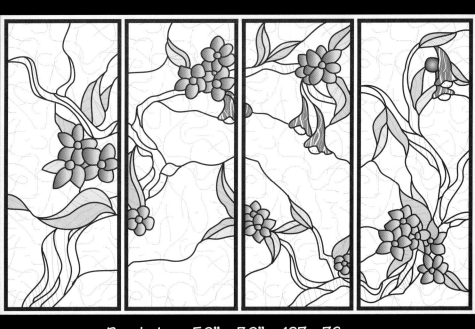

Panel size - 50" x 30" – 127 x 76 cm

Panel size - 50" x 30" – 127 x 76 cm

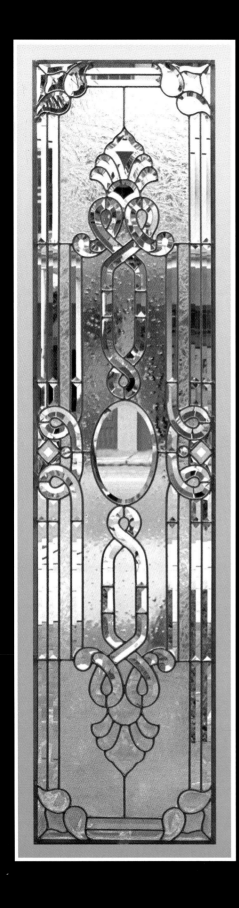

"Art glass panels add both privacy and atmosphere to the bath area" – C.H.

Top Panel size
40" x 30" – 101.6 x 76.2 cm

Middle Panel size
40" x 46" – 101.6 x 116.8 cm

Bottom Panel size
40" x 20"
101.6 x 50.8 cm

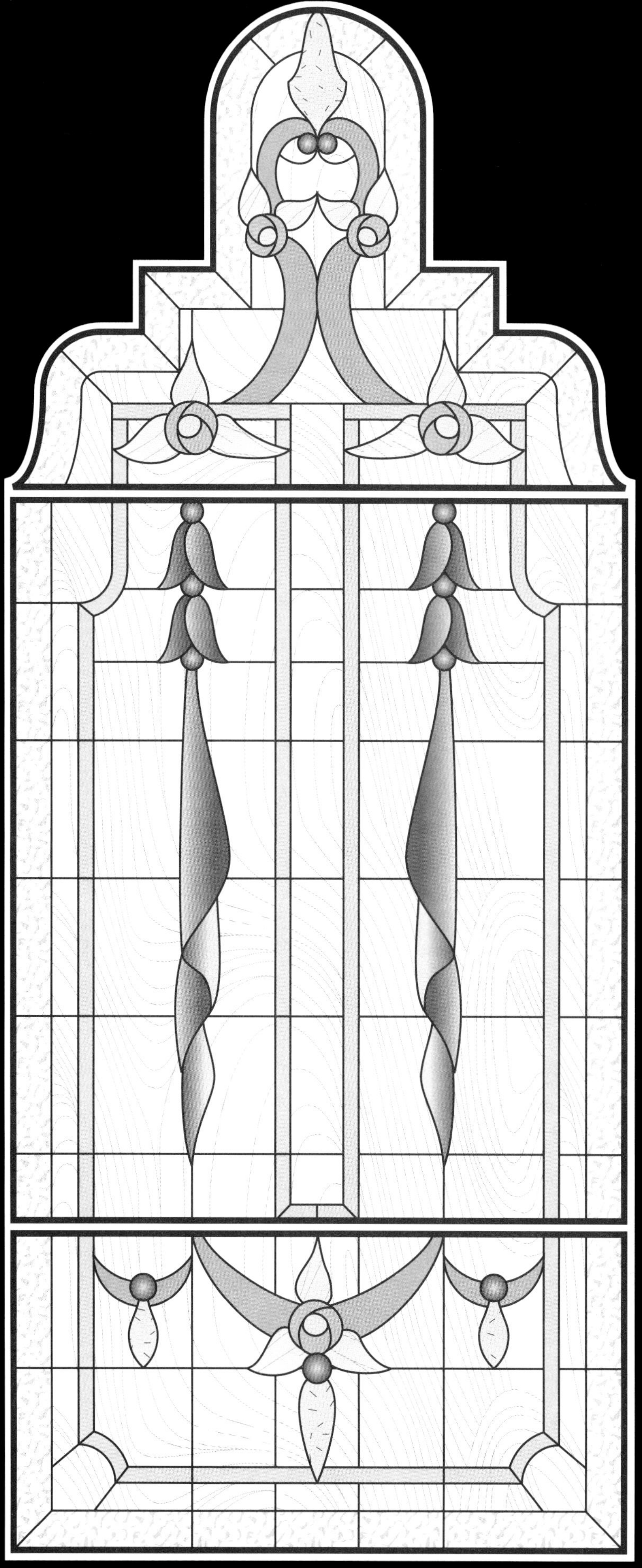

Scale 1" = 10" (10% of full)

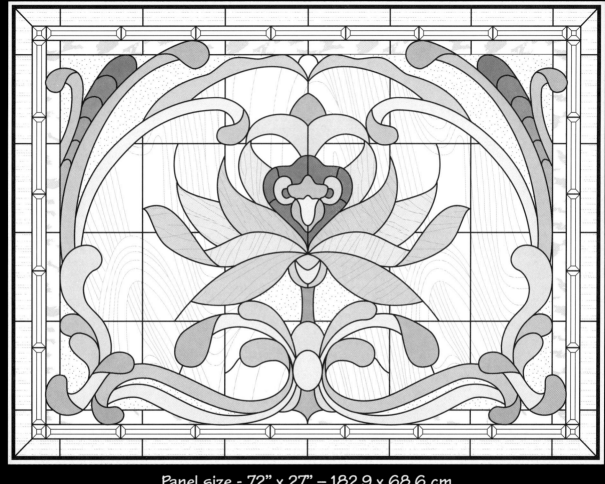

Panel size - 72" x 27" – 182.9 x 68.6 cm

Scale: 1 cm = 10 cm (10% of full-size)

"These stylized traditional designs were fabricated entirely from custom bevels" – C.H.

"Privacy and brilliance has been added to this entry by using a combination of clear textured glass and bevels" – C.H.

"A combination of stock and custom bevels is used to create the oriental theme in these entryway designs" – C.H.

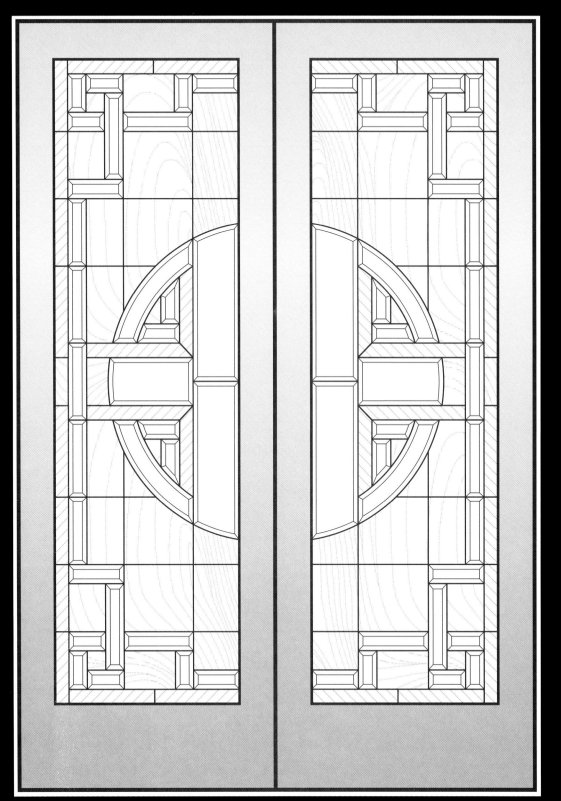

Door Panel size - 28" x 80" – 71.1 x 203.2 cm

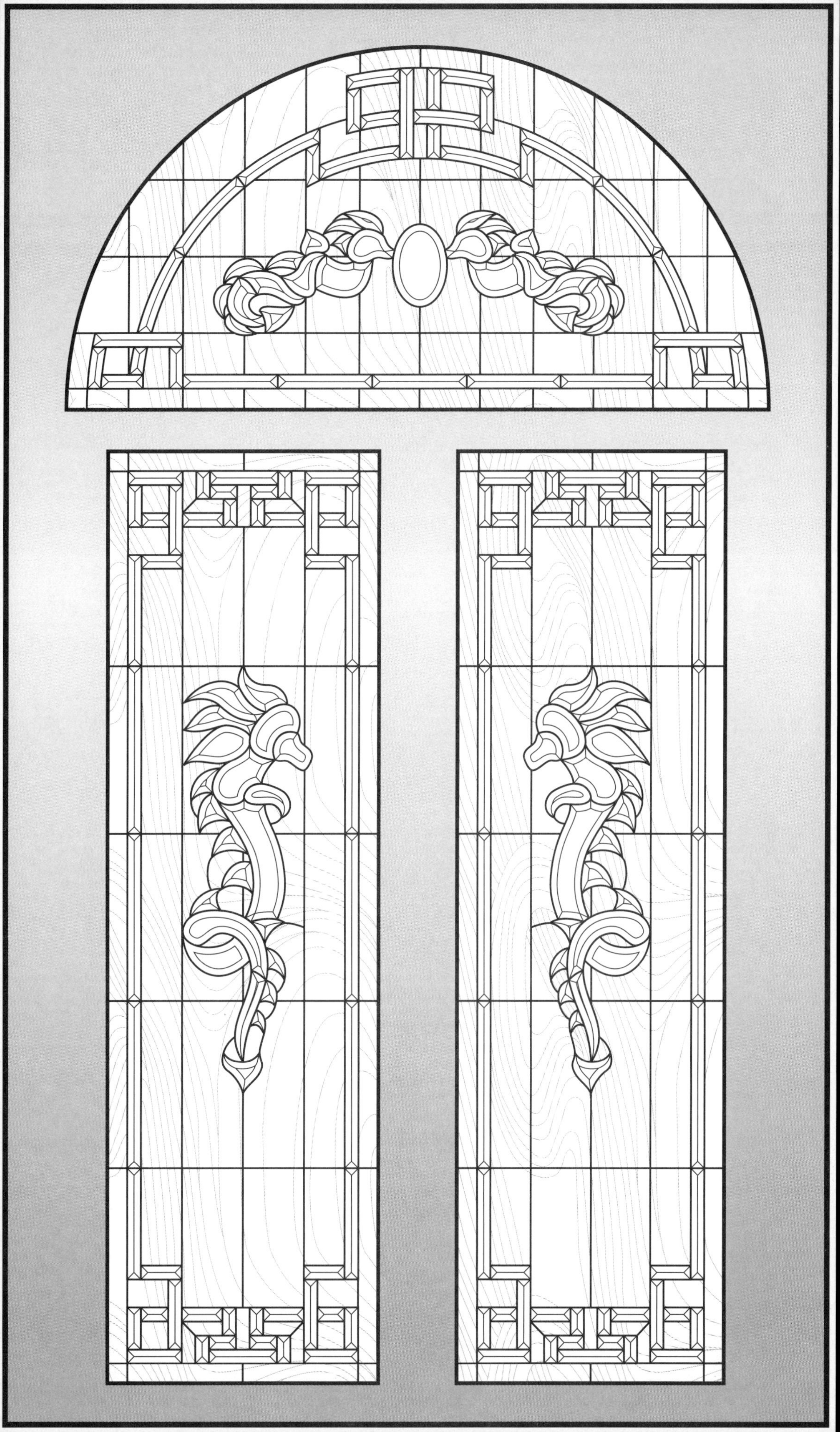

Transom Panel size - 52" x 26" – 132 x 66 cm

Door Panel size - 20" x 67" – 50.8 x 170.2 cm

"These one-piece "Z" shapes push the technical limits of glass" – C.H.

"This contemporary entryway uses 4" x 4" pyramid shaped glass jewels as the main feature of the design" – C.S.

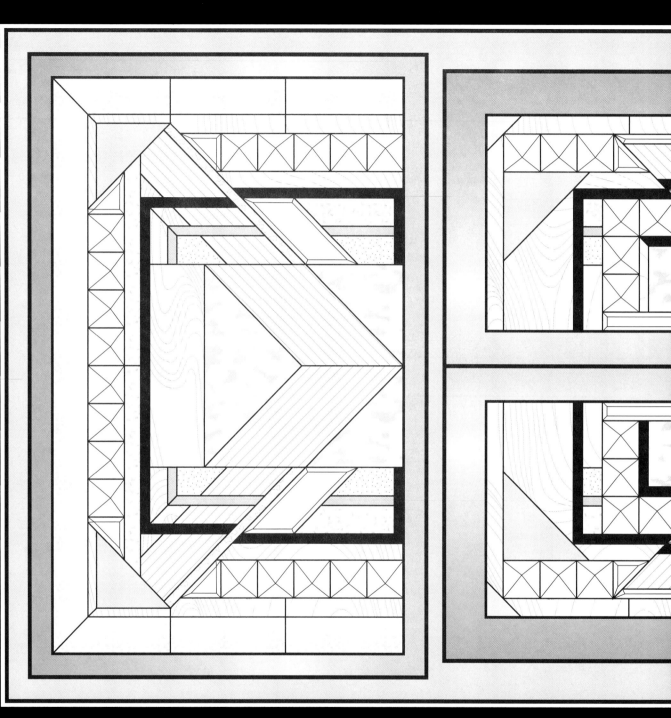

Transom Panel size - 60" x 38" – 152.4 x 96.5 cm

Scale: 1" = 10" / 1 cm = 10 cm (10% of full-size)

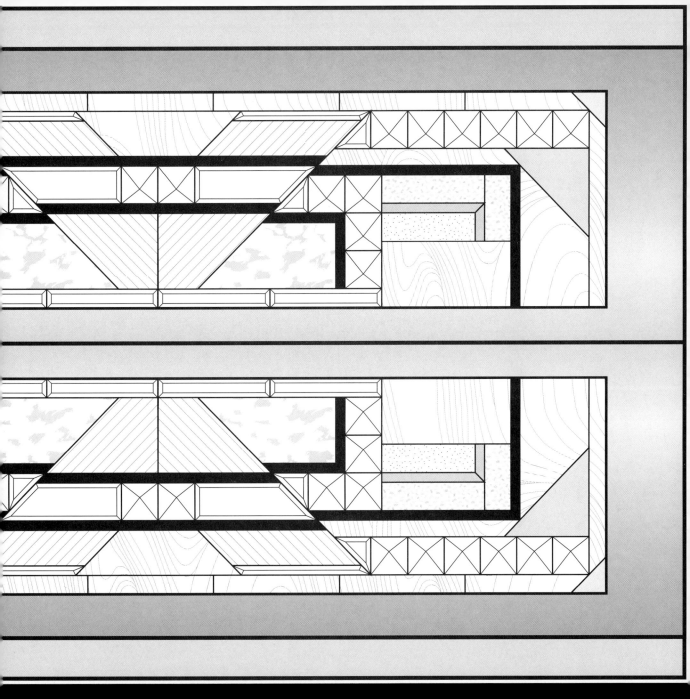

Door Panel size - 22-1/2" x 85" — 57.2 x 215.9 cm

Overall Entryway size (including frame) - 70" x 145" — 177.8 x 368.3 cm

"These doors compliment the same home as the entry on the cover, in addition to the kitchen cabinets and the wall unit on page 45 " – D.K.

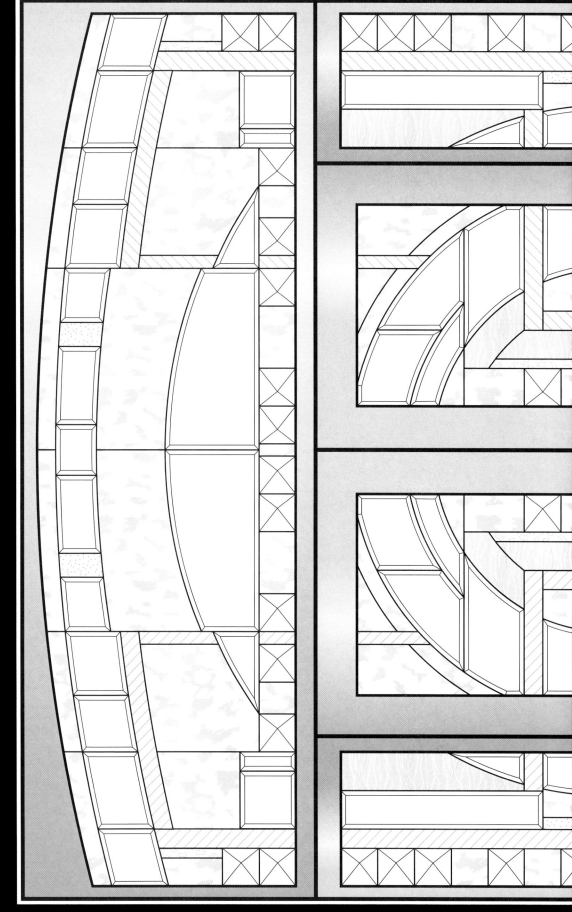

Turn to page 28 to see a photograph of an entryway adapted from this design.

Transom Panel size - 114" x 18-1/2" – 289.6 x 47 cm

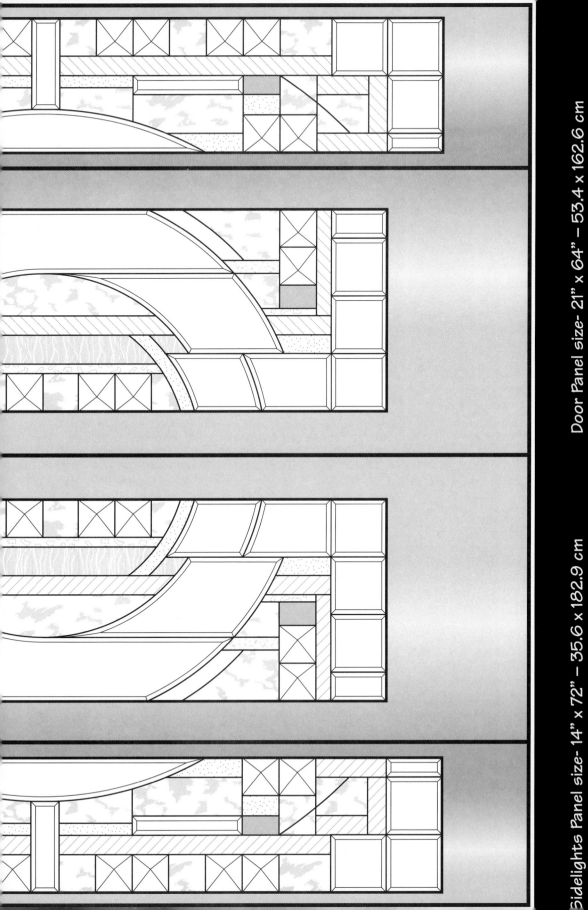

Sidelights Panel size- 14" x 72" – 35.6 x 182.9 cm

Door Panel size- 21" x 64" – 53.4 x 162.6 cm

Overall Entryway size (including frame) - 94" x 116" – 230.8 x 294.6 cm

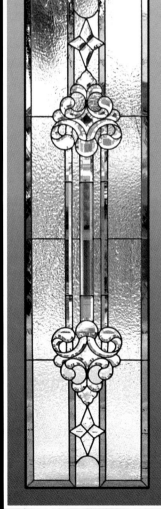

"The central bevel design in these doors was made up from a single stock bevel cluster which we split and then added some custom bevels to create an elegant entryway. The transom uses the same central cluster enhanced with some additional custom bevels" – C.S.

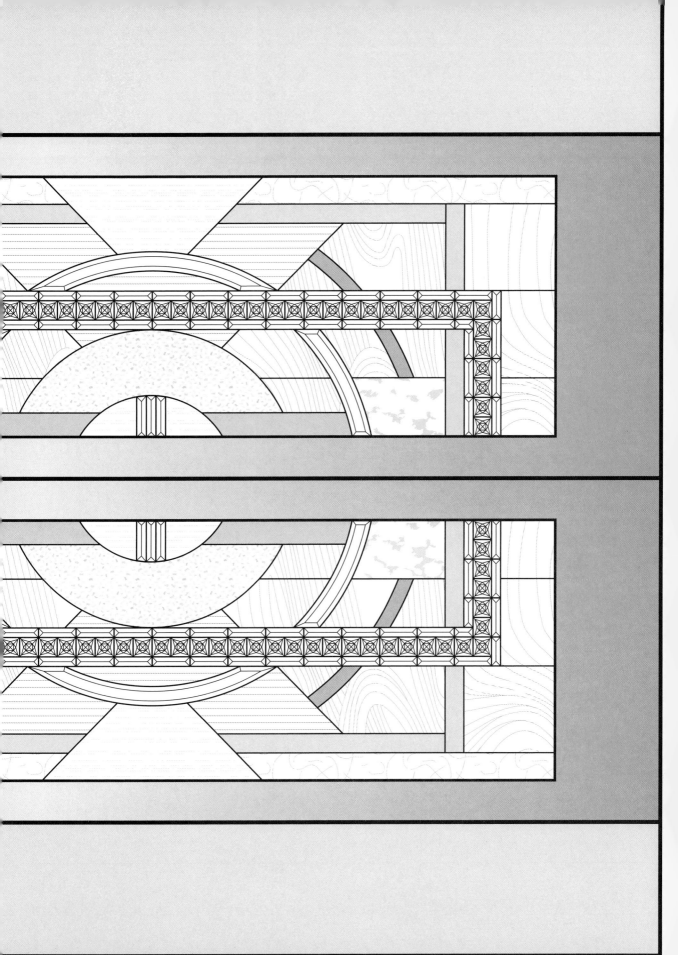

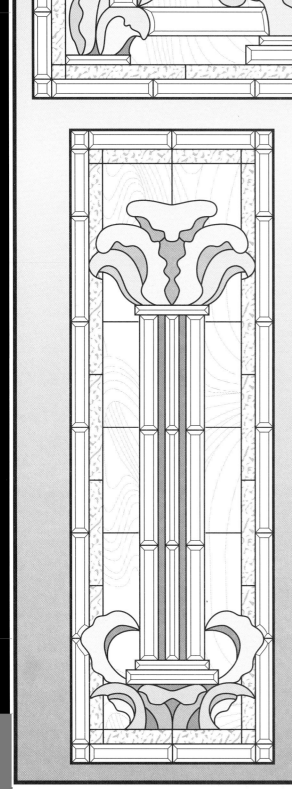
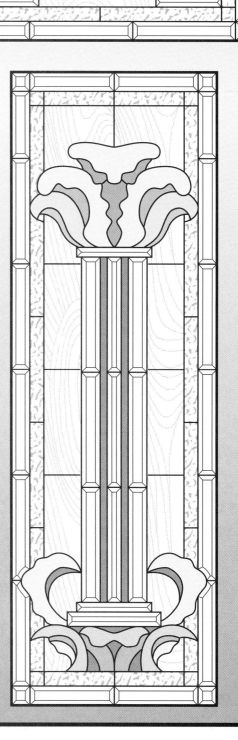

Transom Panel size - 56" x 32" – 142.3 x 81.3 cm

Door Panel size - 21" x 63" – 53.4 x 160 cm

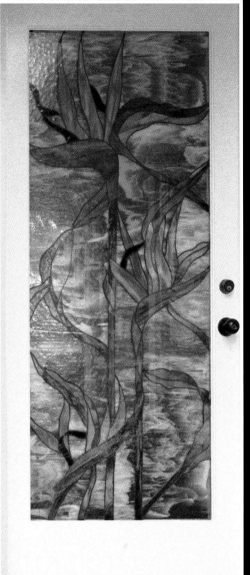

" This tropical inspired design is installed in a water-front restaurant" – C.H.

45

Overall Entryway size (including frame) - 97" x 131" – 246.4 x 332.8 cm

Transom Panel size - 61" x 29" – 154.9 x 73.7 cm

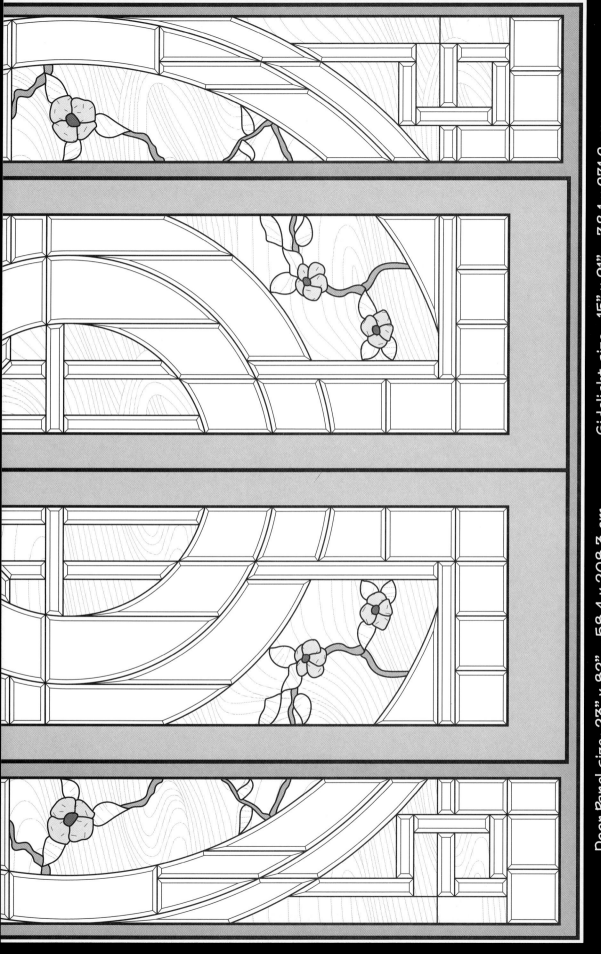

Door Panel size- 23" x 82" – 58.4 x 208.3 cm   Sidelight size - 15" x 91" – 38.1 x 231.2 cm

"This is the original proposal drawing for the entryway pictured on the cover, if you compare the two you will find many changes that were made to the final design." – C.H.

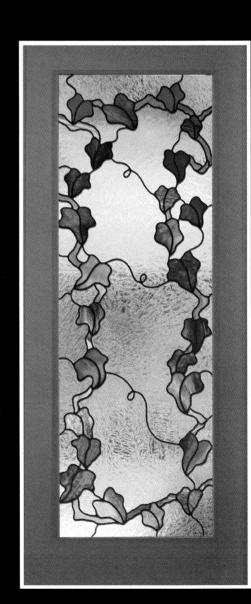

"This 8' x 10' room divider is one of five
areas we constructed for the lobby of
The Sun Bank Corporation – C.H.

"This L.C. Tiffany inspired piece was fabricated in four separate panels that were installed in sliding pocket-wall frames" – C.S.

"We enjoyed the challenge of this 16' x 9' ecclesiastical window. Our thanks to Jackie Gerster for her painting skills on this project" – C.H.

Transom Panel size - 70" x 20" – 177.8 x 50.8 cm

Door Panel size - 22" x 55" – 55.9 x 139.7 cm

You will find a color photograph of these two panels on page 61, bottom.

Panel sizes (all the same) - 23" x 45" – 58.4 x 114.3 cm

"We etched the loon feathers into black on white flashed glass" – C.H.

This design was inspired by a European ceiling painting – D.K. The exquisite glass painting was skillfully done by Crys Soderholm

The gazebo that inspired this panel is on historic Riverwalk in Fort Lauderdale and was the romantic location of the wedding engagement for our clients" – C.H.

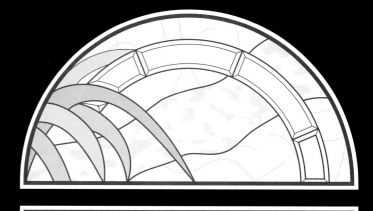

Panel size - 20" x 90"
50.8 x 228.6 cm

Panel size - 35" x 58"
88.9 x 147.3 cm

Scale: 1" = 10" (10% of full-size)

Turn to page 61, top right to see a color photograph of this design

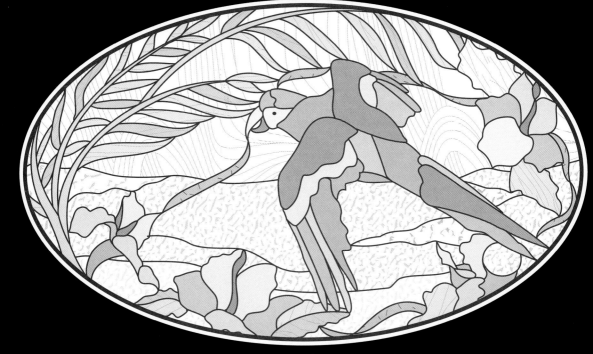

Panel size - 60" x 35" – 152.4 x 88.9 cm

Panel size - 24" x 40" – 61 x 101.6 cm

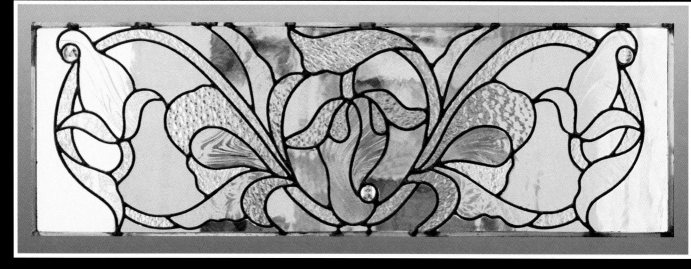

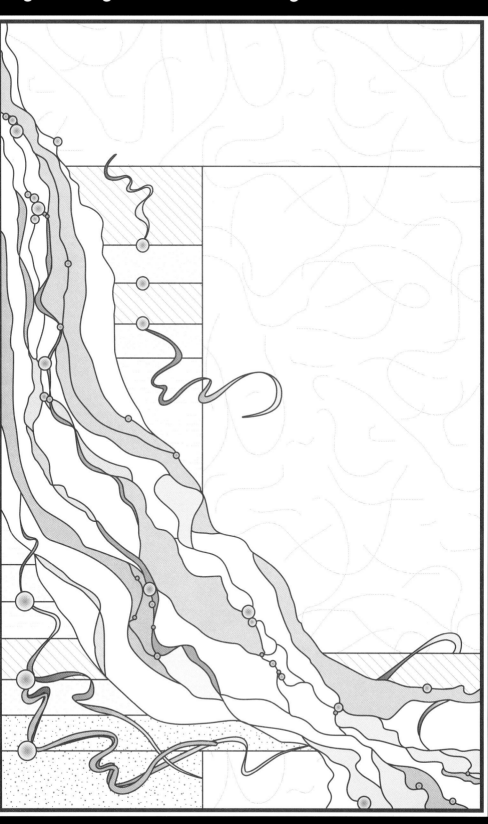

Panel size - 52" x 82" – 132 x 208.2 cm

Turn to page 53 for a color photograph of this design.

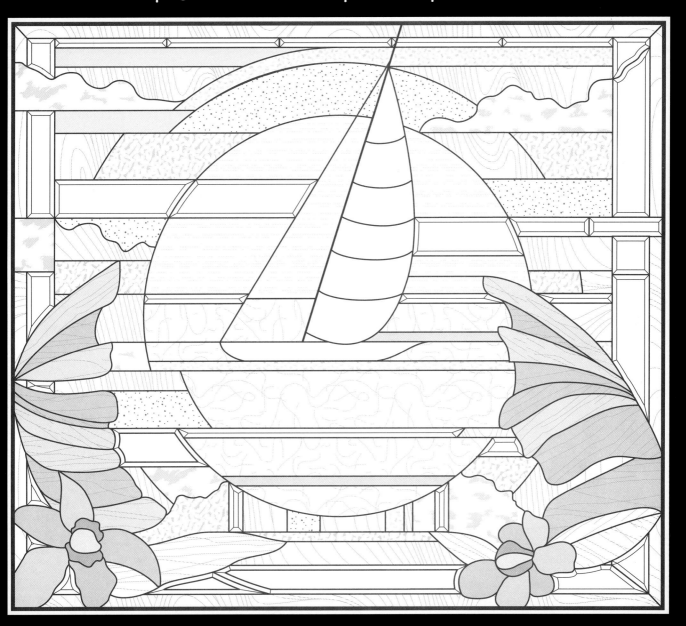

Panel size - 70" x 61" – 177.8 x 154.9 cm

" I delight in breaking-up a more traditional design, like this sailboat scene, by using bevels in unconventional ways throughout the piece" – C.S.

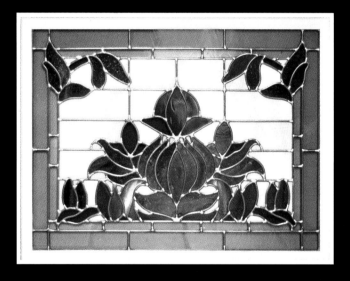

"Since we live near the beach, the ocean and the tropics inspire many of our creations" – C.H.

"This "Key West" influenced design was installed as the focal point of a bar in a private home" – D.K.

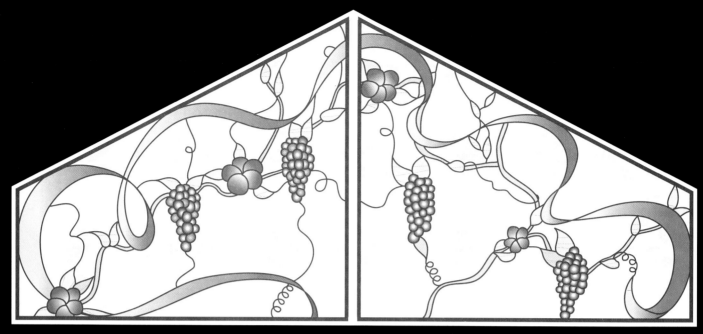

Overall Panel size - 73" x 32" – 185.4 x 81.3 cm

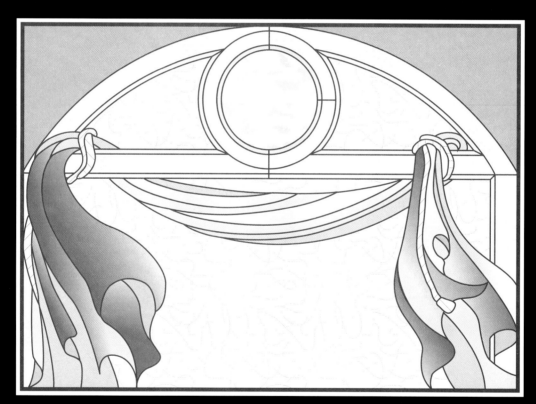

Panel size - 53.5" x 38" – 135.9 x 96.5 cm

"This is one of the proposal designs for a restaurant project. See page 73 for a photograph of the design that the client ultimately chose" – C.S.

Scale: 1" = 10" / 1 cm = 10 cm (10% of full-size)

"This romantic window has roses trailing off into ribbons to form a double heart design" – D.K.

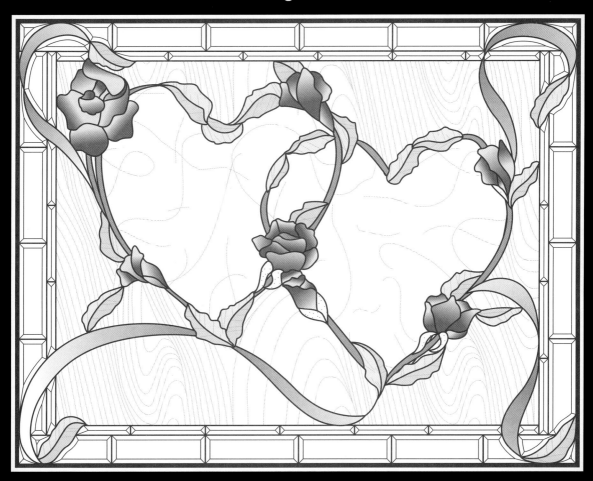

Panel size - 60-1/2" x 46-1/2" – 153.7 x 118.1 cm

Las Palmas Pub

Panel size - 72" x 28" – 183.9 x 71.1 cm

"We were delighted to be chosen as the fabricator of this window for the dining room on a cruise ship" – C.H.

"We used 2300 hand spun rondels
in 15 panels for this project" – C.H.

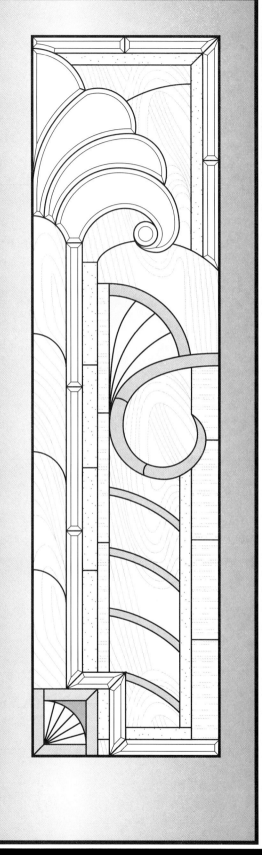

Door Panel size - 20" x 75" – 50.8 x 190.5 cm

The design below and on the opposite page were influenced by the art deco revival that is all the rage here in south Florida. – C.S.
See page 73 for a color photo of a version of this design.

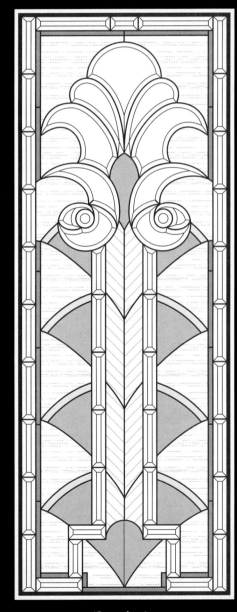

Panel size
22-1/2" x 60-1/2"
57.2 x 153.7 cm

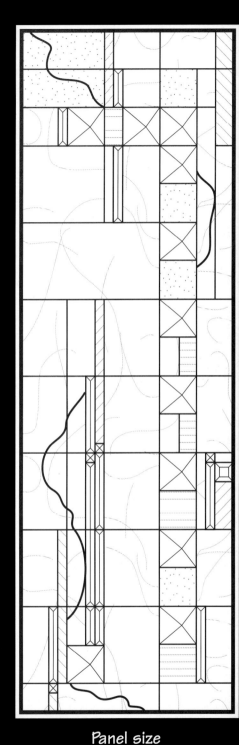

Panel size
23" x 71"
58.4 x 180.4 cm

"I love the effect created when using blown antique glass, bevels and jewels in an abstract combination." C.H.

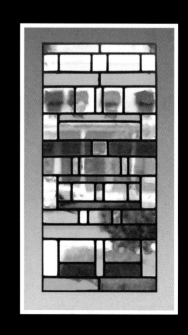

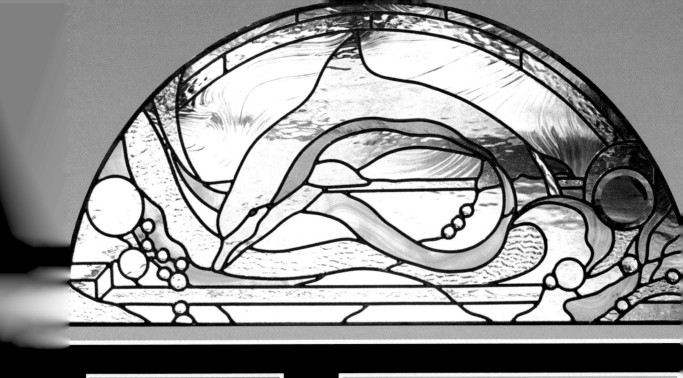

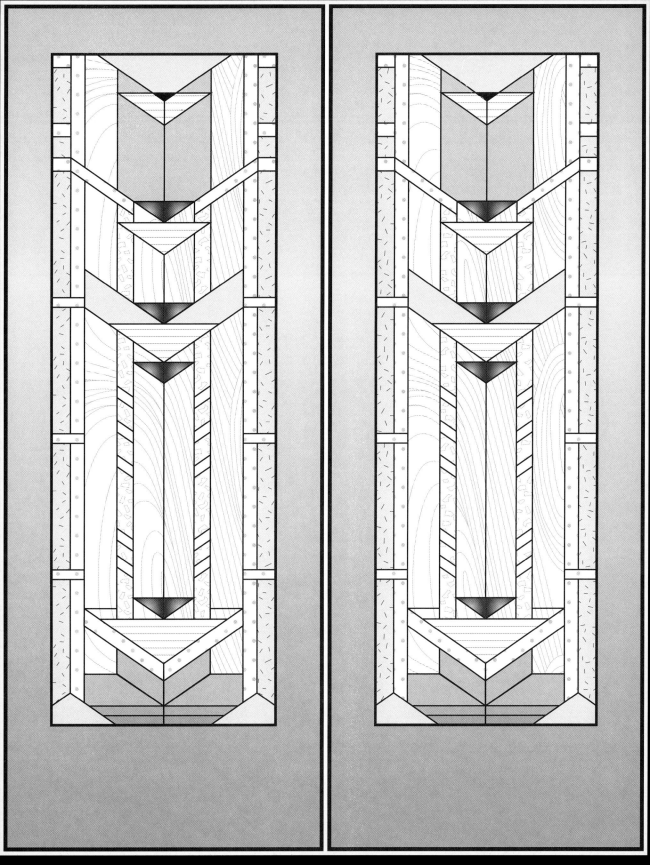

Door Panel size - 20" x 70" – 61 x 177.8 cm

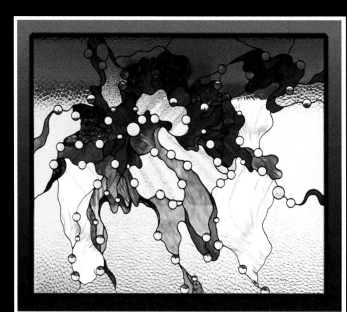

"This panel is made entirely from antique glass for a client in the Caribbean" – C.H.

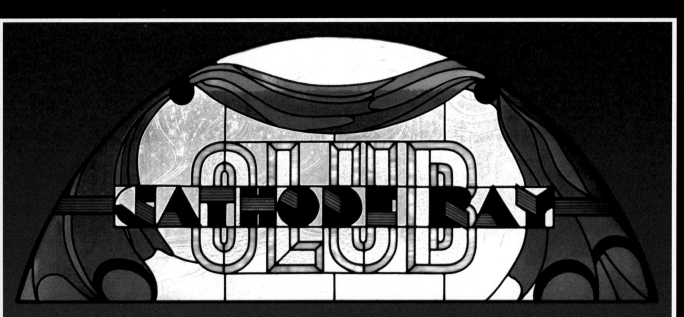

Door Panel size - 22" x 67" – 55.9 x 170.2 cm

Scale: 1" = 10" / 1 cm = 10 cm (10% of full-size)

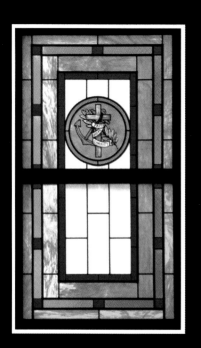

"The hand painted panels from Bovard Studio Inc. are the focal point for these ecclesiastical windows" – C.H.

"We were excited to received this, our very first, church commission depicting the apostolic symbols. The pastor and church committee were a pleasure to work with and their enthusiasm was inspirational" – C.H.

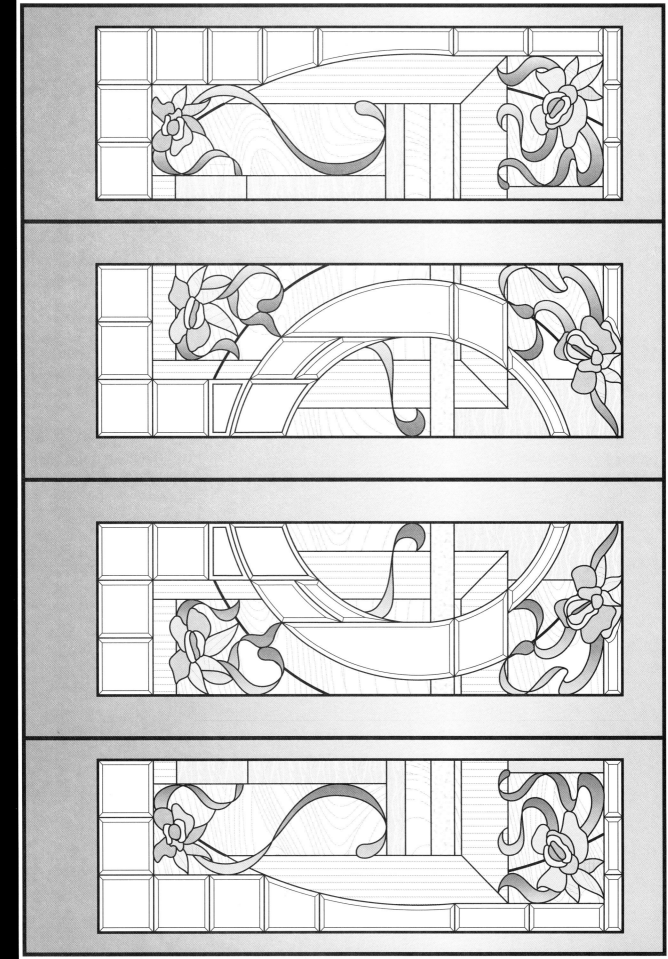

The Wardell Publications Stained Glass Library

INTRODUCTION TO STAINED GLASS by Wardell   70 pages   17 Patterns   ISBN 0-919985-04-1

A comprehensive do-it-yourself manual providing in-depth step-by-step information on tools, supplies and techniques. Instructions include pattern making, glass cutting, fitting, soldering, and finishing for both copper foil and lead came assembly. Lamp making and other special techniques are also covered. 17 project patterns are included ranging from sun-catchers, boxes and small windows to stained glass swag & table lampshades.

QUICK SUCCESS STAINED GLASS by Wardell   48 pages   18 Patterns   ISBN 0-919985-18-1

This all color instruction book is designed to get new crafters up and running as quickly as possible. The quick read format makes learning stained glass craft techniques simple and fun. 18 full-size patterns. Detailed safety guides throughout the book.

LAMPSHADE PATTERNS I by Wardell   48 pages   22 Patterns   ISBN 0-919985-00-9

Full-size patterns for 22 shades ranging in diameter from 5" to 16". All are shown in color, matched with an appropriate lampbase.

MORE LAMPSHADE PATTERNS II by Wardell   28 pages   11 Patterns   ISBN 0-919985-05-X

Step-by-step instructions and full-size patterns for 11 large swag-style shades. The designs include six dining room lamps (16" to 22") a 15" x 27" pool table lamp and four (14" to 19") living room styles. All projects shown in full color.

DESIGNS FOR LAMPS by C. Knapp   48 pages   18 Patterns   ISBN 0-919985-06-8

An exciting collection of full-size patterns for 18 lampshades from 6" to 15" in diameter. These shades were designed primarily to be mounted on a lampbase and information to help match the base to shade is provided.

DESIGNS FOR LAMPS II by C. Knapp   46 pages   29 Patterns   ISBN 0-919985-23-8

Once again Charles Knapp has put together an innovative collection of 22 lampshade patterns from his prolific drawing board. Charles has gone "retro" with his style in this book and has given us more of the designs that made the original Designs for Lamps so highly regarded.

LAMPWORKS by 5 designers   46 pages   16 Patterns   ISBN 0-919985-14-9

Lamp patterns, by five different designers, include 3 inverted ceiling lampshades, 4 table-lamps and 9 swag lamps. Some incorporate bevels and for a challenge, an elaborate 24" diameter old rose dining room lamp. Assembly instructions included.

NORTHERN SHADES by 6 designers   46 pages   25 Patterns   ISBN 0-919985-17-3

The 25 full-size lampshade designs range from small night-stand styles, to elaborate dining room show pieces. Included are 3 wall sconces, which are convertible to medium swag shades for matching lamp sets. You will also find 2 of the popular inverted ceiling style shades. Most shades are medium sized, suitable for either swag or lampbase applications. Color photographs and instructions

STAINED GLASS BOXES by Wardell   68 pages   34 Patterns   ISBN 0-919985-01-7

34 patterns for the popular stained glass jewelry box. The design styles include a sailboat, antique car, geometrics, mini ring boxes & a storage box for audio cassettes. The simple assembly steps are fully explained and all boxes are shown in color.

TERRARIUMS & PLANTERS by Wardell   68 pages   30 Patterns   ISBN 0-919985-02-5

This comprehensive book contains a wide range of designs for 30 plant containers. The step-by-step assembly instructions are accompanied by a helpful guide to selecting and caring for plants in terrariums. All projects are photographed in color.

WALL DECORATIONS by Wardell   68 pages   29 Patterns   ISBN 0-919985-03-3

This book contains 29 patterns for assorted clocks, mirrors & picture frames. Projects include a 30" high granddaughter clock, 11", 22" & 29" oval mirrors, a pendulum schoolhouse clock and much more. All are shown in color with instructions.

CLASSIC ALPHABETS by T. Martin   48 pages   8 Patterns   ISBN 0-919985-13-X

This book contains three complete alphabet styles and two numeral styles. There are 20 line drawings of project ideas for use in stained glass or sand-etching. Information on creating a full-size drawing, dividing the background and use of color. 8 full-size patterns for signs, frames, etc.

MIRRORS & FRAMES by Wardell   52 pages   43 Patterns   ISBN 0-919985-15-7

27 full-size patterns for mirror frames, plus 16 glass overlay designs which can be combined in an almost countless number of ways. The instruction section includes working with mirror glass, adjusting patterns, sealing the mirror edge and important tips for preventing "creeping black edge".

CLOCK GALLERY by Wardell   52 pages   18 Patterns   ISBN 0-919985-16-5

A stained glass book dedicated to clocks. Patterns include a 31" high grandfather clock, a school house regulator plus several floral wall-mounted & traditional free-standing clocks. The how-to section has valuable information on clock movement installation, metal clock faces, bezels and pendulum bob adjustments.

ART GLASS INSPIRATIONS by S. CANN   42 pages   32 Patterns   ISBN 0-919985-20-3

32 Free-form designs for window lightners of sports figures, pets, flowers and birds plus 5 fan lamp designs. An exciting feature of the designs in this collection is the surface paint effects. An extensive how-to section explains the simple painting technique using a special transfer paper that is included with the book.

BEVEL WINDOW DESIGNS by Wardell   72 pages   114 Drawings   ISBN 0-919985-07-6

This book has 32 color photographs and over 100 detailed line drawings of beveled glass windows offering a broad range of design styles including traditional, floral, birds, landscapes, and much more. How-to methods for pattern enlarging, custom designing, framing and more. A book of inspirations.

WINDOWS OF DISTINCTION by McMow Art Glass Designers   80 pages   110 Color photographs   45 Drawings   ISBN 0-919985-22-X

This book contains more than 150 stained glass window designs. The collection is drawn from the studio designer's portfolio of McMow Art Glass covering more than 18 years of commissions. Styles include all aspects of leaded glass design from beveled panels to landscape but the spectacular entryways are particularly outstanding. This is an essential book for all art glass libraries and will appeal to architects, builders, interior designers and all stained glass enthusiasts.

WINDOWS OF ELEGANCE by Glass Reflections Designers   80 pages   108 Color photographs   48 Drawings   ISBN 0-919985-21-1

This design studio portfolio contains over 150 designs for stained glass windows. The photographs and drawings are from the designer archive at Glass Reflections of Fort Lauderdale. The array of design styles include traditional, tropical, floral, beveled panels, modern abstracts, landscapes, and magnificent entryways. This book is indispensible in all art glass libraries and will appeal to architects, builders, interior designers and all stained glass enthusiasts

WINDOWS OF NORTH AMERICA a collection of Nine Studios   80 pages   108 Color photographs   48 Drawings   ISBN 0-919985-24-6

Take a tour of nine renowned art glass studios located throughout the USA and across Canada. This book contains one of the most inspiring collections of designer glass ever assembled. Each studio is featured in an 8 page layout presenting color photographs of spectacular installations and artists proposals. This book will be a valued addition to all art glass libraries and is essential for architects, interior designers, glass artists and everyone who appreciates beautiful glass.

WINDOWS OF VISION by Leslie Perlis Designer   80 pages   81 Photographs   43 Drawings   ISBN 0-919985-29-7

Leslie Perlis's art glass creations have been delighting both public and private spaces for more than 25 years. The collection of images in this book is a selected overview from her portfolio of work. You will find over 66 color photographs, 43 detailed line drawings and 15 grayscale images chronicling her diverse styles. Her commitment to artistic excellence while pushing the technical envelope is in evidence throughout this collection.

Wardell
PUBLICATIONS INC

FULL SIZE
LAMPSHADE PATTERNS I
MINI TO MEDIUM SIZED SHADES

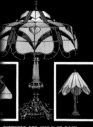

PATTERNS FOR SWAG OR BASE
PHOTOGRAPH OF EACH COMPLETED PROJECT
STEP BY STEP LESSONS — TRADE SECRETS

MORE
LAMPSHADE PATTERNS II
TO 22" DIAMETER SHADES

FULL-SIZE PATTERNS FOR
11 UNIQUE DESIGNS

STEP INSTRUCTIONS — LAMPFORMS **NOT** REQUIRED

CHARLES KNAPP
DESIGNS FOR LAMPS
FOR 18 SMALL TO MEDIUM SHADES

Charles Knapp
DESIGNS FOR LAMPS II
Patterns For 22 Small to Medium Shades

22 FULL-SIZE LAMPSHADE PATTERNS FOR 5" to 12" DIAMETER SHADES
LAMPSHADE STYLES INCLUDE • TABLES • SWAGS • MINIS
INCLUDES A COMPLETE STEP-BY-STEP GUIDE TO LAMPSHADE CONSTRUCTION

WARDELL PUBLICATIONS • STUDIO DESIGNER SERIES
Stained Glass
Windows of Elegance
Collection Two

Featuring
Glass Publications
of Worr Labarriere
STUDIO DESIGNERS

WARDELL PUBLICATIONS • STUDIO DESIGNER SERIES
Stained Glass
Windows of Distinction
Collection One

Featuring
McMow Art Glass

WARDELL PUBLICATIONS • STUDIO DESIGNER SERIES
Stained Glass
Windows of North America
Collection Three

WARDELL PUBLICATIONS • STUDIO DESIGNER SERIES
Stained Glass
Windows of Vision
Collection Four

featuring
Leslie Perlis
Studio

NORTHERN SHADES
95 FULL-SIZE PATTERNS FOR STAINED GLASS LAMPSHADES

PATTERNS FOR 5" TO 21" DIAMETER SHADES - STYLES INCLUDE:
INVERTED CEILINGS • WALL SCONCES • TABLES • SWAG
STEP INSTRUCTIONS - LAMPFORMS **NOT** REQUIRED

LAMPWORKS
FULL-SIZE PATTERNS FOR STAINED GLASS LAMPSHADES

DESIGN STYLES FOR 10" TO 24" DIAMETER SHADES
STEP INSTRUCTIONS—LAMPFORMS **NOT** REQUIRED

QUICK SUCCESS
STAINED GLASS
BEGINNER'S INSTRUCTION GUIDE

QUICK SUCCESS
STAINED GLASS
A BEGINNER'S INSTRUCTION GUIDE

INTRODUCTION TO
STAINED GLASS
A TEACHING MANUAL

A COMPLETE HOW-TO-DO STAINED GLASS MANUAL
INCLUDING FULL-SIZE PATTERNS FOR 17 PROJECTS

32 FULL-SIZE FREE-FORM DESIGNS FOR
ART GLASS
INSPIRATIONS

32 FULL-SIZE PATTERNS
FOR FREE-FORM
WINDOW LIGHTENERS

COMPLETE STEP-BY-STEP GUIDE
TO DETAIL PAINTING USING
SMALL TRACING PAPER
INCLUDED WITH THIS BOOK
IT'S EASY TO TRANSFER THE
DESIGN FOR AIR-DRY ENAMEL
PAINT APPLICATION

STAINED GLASS
WALL DECORATIONS
PATTERNS FOR CLOCKS,
MIRRORS AND PICTURE FRAMES

DESIGNS FOR 29 COMPLETE PROJECTS
STEP-BY-STEP INSTRUCTION

STAINED GLASS
CLOCK GALLERY

• FULL-SIZE PATTERNS FOR 36 CLOCKS
• STEP-BY-STEP INSTRUCTIONS

Classic Alphabets
by Tammie Martin

FULL-SIZED ALPHABETS & NUMERALS

SIX COMPLETE ALPHABETS IN THREE DIFFERENT FONT STYLES
Detailed techniques for designing with letters
20 Design drawings and 8 full-sized project patterns

Bevel Window Designs
INSPIRATIONS FOR LEADED
GLASS WINDOWS

DESIGN DRAWINGS
PHOTOGRAPHS
INCLUDE TRADITIONAL
LANDSCAPE
VICTORIAN and
CONTEMPORARY ABSTRACT

Patterns for
Stained Glass
BOXES

FULL-SIZE PATTERNS FOR 34 ART GLASS BOXES
Basic assembly techniques, including hinge installation

PATTERNS FOR
MIRRORS
& FRAMES

• FULL-SIZE PATTERNS FOR 47 MIRRORS
AND 16 GLASS OVERLAYS
• STEP-BY-STEP INSTRUCTIONS
• Important Tips for Care
and Cleaning of Mirror
• Design Ideas Drawings for
More Project Construction

PATTERNS FOR
TERRARIUMS
& PLANTERS

DESIGNS FOR 30 COMPLETE PROJECTS
GUIDE TO SELECTION AND CARE OF PLANTS
STEP-BY-STEP INSTRUCTION

E-mail: info@wardell
publications.com
Website: www.
wardellpublications.com